So You Want To Be A Flight Attendant

HerJourney Publishing Company, Inc.

Phone: 1-877-648-6597

www.hjpbooks.com

All HerJourney titles, imprints, and distributed lines are available at special quantity discounts for bulk purchases for sales promotion, premiums, fund raising, educational, or institutional use.

Special book excerpts or customized printings can also be created to fit specific needs. For details, email or phone the office of the

HerJourney Sales Manager:

Attn. Special Sales Department.

Phone: 1-877-648-6597

hjpbooks@gmail.com

ISBN-10: 0-9859330-5-4
ISBN-13: 978-0-9859330-5-0

So You Want To Be A Flight Attendant

PREFACE

If you:

Thought about becoming a Flight Attendant

Are looking for a career change

Want to travel the World

Just thought it would be interesting

This book is for you. This book's job is to inform you of things most people don't know before making the decision to become a Flight Attendant.

Each year, thousands of people wonder if becoming a Flight Attendant is for them. Some even spend thousands of dollars and countless hours in Flight Attendant training schools pursuing this dream only to find out it isn't exactly what they were looking for and not even close. By then, they've already uprooted their lives.

I want to give you an intimate look into the Flight Attendant world and let you make an informed decision for yourself without investing large amounts of money and time.

I've been flying for many years and I want to help any newcomers in their quest to become a Flight Attendant. I thoroughly enjoy my job and want to make sure that every one of you knows exactly what it takes to get into this industry as well as what to expect once you're hired.

Most people that quit do so within the first 6 months. There are a myriad of reasons. This book will give you a heads up about things that drive most people out. Once in the door, if you can stick it out for the first year of flying, you have made it.

I hope this book helps.

Sincerely,

Kay Jay ♥

1. Do I Have What It Takes?

Do I mind spending most of my day in a metal tube?

-The majority of a Flight Attendant's day is spent on a plane. If you are afraid of small, enclosed spaces (**claustrophobia**) or afraid of heights (**acrophobia**), this job is *NOT* for you at this time. I encourage you to conquer those fears and then move forward with becoming a Flight Attendant.

*Imagine if you will you're on a flight and your Flight Attendant is visibly shaken by such things. Would you feel safe?

Am I willing to be away from my family for long periods of time?

-Becoming a Flight Attendant requires long periods away from home at times. **Missing important days like birthdays and holidays** will also be a requirement. Especially in the beginning. If you are able to be away from your family and friends for extended periods of time, you are one step closer to becoming a Flight Attendant.

*I once knew a Flight Attendant who hadn't made it home in the 5 months after she'd been hired because flights were always full to her home city and she was on reserve. That takes dedication.

Am I willing to live in another city?

-Often an airline will not have a **domicile** or **base** (your assigned city to work from) in the city you live in. You will have to decide whether to move to the city you are assigned to or commute to work.

Once, I packed up and moved to my base after 3 years of flying because I was tired of commuting. These are the choices you may have to make.

Am I willing to commute to work?

-If you do not live in the base your Company assigned you and you have chosen not to move, you will be considered a **commuter**. Commuting is the act of traveling between your home and base on a regular basis. Most Flight Attendants commute using airplanes, but others that live close enough to base may chose to drive, ride the bus or train. There are many ways to get to work and you have to choose which one works best for you.

-Commuting is not always easy and can be very stressful at times. If you are relying on airplane travel to commute you will most likely be **Non-Revving**. Non-Revving is traveling as a standby employee on a plane. You will get a seat once the plane is full of all revenue paying passengers. If there are seats left on the plane, you will then board in order of **seniority or check-in,** as there will probably be more Non-

Revs trying to board that flight as well. We will discuss seniority later.

I commuted from Houston to several different bases for 4 years. That was a LOT of time spent on planes and in airport.

Am I willing to take a pay cut?

-Even though most Flight Attendants make this job look super glamorous it can take a toll. One of the things that shock most new Flight Attendants is the pay. Starting out at most airlines, you will take a pay cut. The pay will vary by airline. *Southwest Airlines is currently the highest paying for Flight Attendants in the U.S.*

This job is not for those who expect to become rich straight out the gate. Flight Attendant pay is not like a normal job. Once you've been here awhile you will become creative with your flying in order to make more money.

Am I a "People Person"?

-In doing this job, you will come into contact with a variety of people. You will need to be able to adapt to different people, places and situations. **Your prejudices will need to be checked at the door in order to do this job properly**.

I come from a military family so it was easier for me to adapt to different people and situations. You will need to be able to interact with everyone with a smile.

Am I flexible enough?

-The name of the game in being a Flight Attendant is **FLEXIBILITY**. Starting out in this job requires a large amount of flexibility. You will be working random hours, holidays, weekends and birthdays until you garner enough seniority.

*I spent my 40th birthday with my crew and that was one of the best birthdays I ever had.

2. How do I get in the door?

Are you at least 21 years old?

-Each airline is different. Most require you to be 21. Some will allow you to be 20, but you have to be 21 by the time you are hired. Check with each airline to make sure. **There is no maximum age limit**. If you can perform the job duties safely and efficiently, you can be a Flight Attendant.

You will be able to serve those oh so popular drinks legally at 21. The oldest person in my initial training class was 65. If you can do the job, it's yours. You can always start working at an airline in another capacity until you've reached the age limit for that company to fly. That way your seniority transfers with you.

Do you have a high school diploma/GED?

-College degrees are not required to become a Flight Attendant with most airlines. A high school diploma/GED is.

It doesn't take a rocket scientist to do this job, but it does take someone who can finish something to the end. Stay in school.

Are you willing to travel to another city for the initial interview?

-Most airlines hold Flight Attendant interviews in different cities. If an interview session is held in another city other than the one you live in, you may be required to pay for your own travel and lodging. In some cases the airline may fly you in for the initial interview.

Here's a tip. Find someone you know with buddy passes for the airplane ticket to your interview and pick an interview city where you know someone so you can possibly crash at their house for a night or two. Where there is a will there is a way. Remember to say Thank You and offer to pay for gas and/or food.

Do you have customer service experience?

-**Customer Service is the name of the game**. During the interview process you will be asked about your Customer Service background. Be prepared with anecdotes (stories) to share with your interviewer. Your resume' should go back **at least** 10 years to satisfy **FAA (Federal Aviation Administration)** requirements. Emphasize your customer service positions on your resume'.

Don't go overboard with the stories. Remember these interviewers do this for a living and they've heard and seen it all. Keep your stories honest, short and add a little humor, if called for.

Are you able to pass a medical exam?

-Some airlines require you to participate in a medical exam to show you are fit enough to perform the duties of a Flight Attendant. You will also be given a drug test.

This may be the time to give up any bad habits you have and start exercising. You don't want your vices to stand in the way of your dream job. Also remember that airlines give extremely random drug tests. I know of a young lady that was fired because she took a drink on her last working flight of the day and there was a random drug test awaiting the crew at the end of the trip.

Have a passport?

-**All airlines require you to have a passport**. You will need to have a passport or be able to show a receipt for a passport during training.

This is self explanatory.

Can I pass a background check?

-It is very important to be truthful on your Flight Attendant application. As mentioned above, the FAA will require personal addresses and job positions for the past **10 years**. If you have gaps of unemployment or homelessness you will need to have an acceptable reason why. Remember to **Be Honest.**

Certain countries we travel to do not allow people in who've exhibited bad behavior in the past or not so distant past. Canada is one of them. You have to be honest because the company you are applying to will find out. I once saw a woman get all the way through training and then her background came back. She didn't get her wings.

3. Interview Time!!

How should I dress?

-Dress should be conservative during the interview process. Be Professional.

- *Black or Dark Blue Suit/Dress*

- *Hose or Dress socks*

- *Clean shoes*

- *Hide your tattoos*

- *Natural hair colors*

- *The only piercings that should show are two small studded earrings for the ladies.*

*I once witnessed a young lady lotion her bare legs with a very strong smelling Victoria Secret lotion during an interview. She did not get the job.

What questions will they ask?

-Please see the Commonly Asked Interview Questions at the end of this book.

Do you have great customer service stories?

-Please see the Commonly Asked Interview Questions at the end of this book.

What are they looking for in the interview?

-During the whole interview process they will be watching you. They want to see how well you interact with the other applicants as well as how you carry yourself in a public setting. You never know who you may be talking to in such settings, so it is always important to be polite and professional.

Some of those people you interview with will become lifelong friends.

What if I can't make it to my interview?

-If you cannot make it to your interview, call well in advance and try to reschedule. Make sure you have a good reason for doing so.

Things happen.

4. I got the job! What's next?

Can you attend training for 3-8 weeks?

-Training length varies by airline. Some Regional airlines are as little as 3 weeks long. A Mainline carrier can go up to 8 weeks. **Be prepared**.

Make sure that you've previously arranged for car notes, rent and other expenses to be taken care of so you can concentrate on training.

Will I be paid for training?

-**Pay for training varies by airline**. Some airlines only pay a per diem. Some have a flat out pay scale. Some airlines pay nothing at all. Prepare accordingly.

You can ask before training starts about pay.

Are you willing to work odd hours?

-**Flight Attendants work extremely odd and long hours**. Some airlines can work up to 16 hour days. There may be days when you work overnight. During training you will be required to work odd hours to give you a taste of what it would be like on the airplane.

When I was in training we were training on planes until 2 a.m. Flight Attendants sometimes have hectic, unplanned schedules due to weather, aircraft maintenance and other unforeseen situations.

Can you perform under pressure?

-This is a question you should answer **honestly**. Training is a time of **significant pressure**. This is done on purpose to see if you can handle strenuous situations that are bound to come your way. There are deadlines that need to be met on flights to ensure **on time arrival and departure**. Not to mention any emergency that may arise while in flight. You also have to remember that you will have hundreds of people's lives in your hands on any given day and you will be counted upon to **respond accordingly**. It can be done and you can do it.

*I've had medical emergencies, extreme turbulence and other situations that required my complete attention and calmness. Everyone on the plane will be looking to you to lead them in strenuous times.

Do you have a problem sharing a room with a stranger?

-Most airlines require you to share a room with another same sex applicant during training. **This is a test** to see how well you adapt to your surroundings. This is where the **"people person" skills** come into play. Remember the Golden Rule. **Treat people how your wish to be treated** and you will be fine.

Communication is paramount when dealing with a roommate that you do not know. Set good rules and boundaries and honor them.

5. I completed training! Now what?

How do I get to my new base?

-Your **base** is the location you will fly in and out of for work. During training you will be asked to list your base preferences in order of most desired to least desired. The Company will then decide where Flight Attendants are needed within their system and assign accordingly. Some of you will start flying directly out of class. Most airlines provide their employees with flight benefits which enables them to **commute** to their new **base**. You will perform your **OE** or **Operating Experience** to let the Company know if you are ready to fly or need more training

Don't panic. As you go through training you will understand the ins and outs of travel. Your trainers will be a great help at this time.

Where will I live?

- As discussed in the previous section you will either become a **commuter** or **live in base**. Although living in base is easier, it is not an option for everyone. You should go into this career with an idea of which option works best for you. **Commuting is a challenge, but it can be done**. The majority of airlines have multiple bases. You won't have to stay in one base forever. Most airlines will let you move to another base as soon as there is an opening.

-Most commuters look for **crashpads**. These are places to live offered by other airline industry people. You use the crashpad when you can't make it home due to weather, missed flights or limited off days. It may be a house, apartment or hotel room that you will be sharing with other flight attendants or pilots. Depending on the set up you could have a room to yourself or share a room with other people.

-Crashpads have cold and hot beds. Cold beds usually cost a little more because it is YOUR designated bed and no one else can use it. Hot beds are for people who just need a place to stay for the night and anyone can use them. Crashpad prices vary and so do their amenities. Once you get to training there are usually plenty of advertisements in the break rooms for crashpads for you to choose from. Call around and make your choice from there.

As I mentioned before, when I started flying I lived in Houston and was based in Louisville. I commuted for 3 years. At some point, I was tired of commuting and decided to switch my base to Philly and moved there. I have lived in a crashpad. There are plenty of pros and cons to such living. The choice is yours.

What is <u>Reserve</u>?

-Reserve is on call flying for Flight Attendants. Each Company has their own way to assign reserve. Most new hires will experience reserve. Length of time on reserve varies by base and airline. You will be paid a **Guarantee** while on reserve. Guarantee is a minimum number of hours the Company automatically pays you even though you may not have flown while on reserve. This is usually a stretch for most Flight Attendants to live on, but it is doable.

Do your research by searching the internet for Flight Attendant chat groups. You will find valuable information and get answers to your many questions about how each airline pays.

What is <u>Seniority</u>?

-**Seniority is crucial in the airline industry**. It could mean getting the last seat on a full flight you are commuting on. The more seniority you have, the easier your life becomes. You start accruing seniority once the Company hires people up under you. Seniority for Flight Attendants means more money and better schedules. Your seniority date is the date you get hired by your airline.

If your company is doing a lot of hiring you will get more seniority quickly. If your company is slow to hire, the opposite will occur.

What is <u>Crew Scheduling</u>?

-Crew Scheduling is the department that makes sure Flight Attendants and Pilots are where they are supposed to be. They are in charge of hotels, transportation and many other things for the crew. You will speak to Crew Scheduling often. Their job is just as demanding as yours.

Crew Schedulers and Flight Attendants have an interesting relationship. Just like Flight Attendants, not all Crew Schedulers are bad people. It pays to know your contract when dealing with them.

A lot of give and take happens with Crew Scheduling. If they ask you to do something extra or that's not already assigned to you, feel free to negotiate with them for something you need and get it in writing.

What is a <u>Probationary Period</u>?

-Most airlines have a period of time where they let the Flight Attendant get use to the Company. Probation varies by airline. It usually lasts anywhere between 3-12 months. **All new Flight Attendants need to be on their best behavior during this period and beyond.**

A lot of unforeseen things can happen while a Flight Attendant is on probation. Be well versed in your contract and utilize your Union as much as possible.

What Contract?

-If you are a Flight Attendant and you belong to a union, you will sign a contract. This contract was voted on by other Flight Attendants before you and was put in place to protect you from possible abuses and misunderstandings. It is important that you understand your contract. If you have questions, most of your fellow Flight

Attendants (or your Union rep) will be glad to help you.

It is important that you understand what your contract is offering you when it is time to vote. Sometimes, Companies will be in the process of voting in a new contract when they are doing mass hiring. This means that people who've never flown before are voting on something that will affect them for a long time. Be sure to get as much information from fellow Flight Attendants and your Union before casting your vote. You don't want to regret your choice down the road.

Airlines

Apply to as many airlines as possible, weigh your options and then make your choice.

International

*- An **international** flight is a form of commercial flight within **civil aviation** where the departure and the arrival take place in different countries. Airports servicing **international** flights are known as **international** airports.*

1. Air Canada 2. Aeromexico 3. British Airways 4. Emirates 5. Qatar Airways 6. Lufthansa 7. Air France	8. KLM 9. Virgin Atlantic 10. Korean Airlines 11. China Airlines 12. South African Airways 13. Alitalia

Mainline

*-A **mainline flights** are operated by an airline's main operating unit, rather than by regional alliances, regional code-shares or regional subsidiaries.*

1. American 2. Delta 3. United 4. Southwest	5. JetBlue 6. Frontier 7. Hawaiian 8. Spirit 9. Virgin America

Regional

-**Regional airlines** are airlines that operate regional aircraft to provide passenger air service to communities without sufficient demand to attract mainline service.

1. Piedmont	9. ExpressJet
2. PSA	10. GoJet Airlines
3. Republic	11. Horizon Air
4. Trans States	12. Mesa
5. Cape Air	13. Air Wisconsin
6. Compass	14. SkyWest
7. Endeavor	
8. Envoy	

Charters

-A **charter** flight is an aircraft in which all the seats are paid for by a travel company and then sold to their customers, usually at a lower cost than that of a scheduled flight. This is usually done by casinos, sports teams and private companies.

Omni
Million Air
NetJets

<u>Commonly Asked Interview Questions</u>

Practice these questions and your answers in the mirror and remember to SMILE. ☺

1. Why do you want to become a Flight Attendant?

2. What makes you think you'd make a great Flight Attendant?

3. What customer service experience do you have?

4. Tell us about a good customer service experience you've had.

5. Tell us about a bad customer service experience you were involved in.

6. Tell us how you handled an upset customer.

7. Tell us about a time when your job was challenging and how you handled it.

8. If you saw a co-worker stealing alcoholic beverages from the service cart, what would you do?

Airport Codes

An IATA **airport code** is also known as an IATA station **code** and is a three-letter **code** designating airports around the world, defined by the International Air Transport Association (IATA).

Each airline requires you to memorize or at least become familiar with airport codes that are frequently used by them. Each airline is different. Familiarize yourself with the lists provided on the website below to give you a head start.

www.airportcodes.org

Things You Will Need Before and During Class

1. Luggage

-Most airlines require an all black roller board the size of 21" – 22" and a black remain over night (RON) bag. You can bring these bags to training and see if they are compliant. If they aren't, most airlines will allow you to purchase luggage through them. Most Flight Attendants tend to over pack. As you learn the job and watch other Flight Attendants, packing will become easier. Check thrift stores for luggage before paying large amounts of money at department stores.

2. What to pack

-You want to pay close attention to the seasons while packing for training. There is nothing like being ill-equipped to fight the elements. You will not be going out and partying as often as you'd think. Studying and training will rule your life during those few weeks. You won't be going home (unless you live nearby) so you want to get this right.

3. Transportation

-Having a car during training is extremely helpful. This is not always possible depending on the location of the training center. People who bring cars are usually the designated driver for a group of people going to places like Wal-Mart, food establishments or the less frequent night out. Some airlines have training compounds with their own transportation for such runs.

4. Food

-Packing food for training is necessary only if you are antisocial and don't plan on making any friends. Most hotels are set up to take you on Wal-Mart/ grocery store runs. As mentioned above, you may want to become friends with people who have transportation.

5. Study Materials

-Most airlines will provide you with all the study materials you need. Some things you will want to bring are pens, pencils, notebooks, highlighters, 3 x 5 cards and sticky notes.

6. Good Shoes

-I went through 4 pairs of shoes in my first year until I realized that comfy shoes are an investment. We're on our feet all day and foot pain is a given. Most airlines require you to have an all leather black or navy blue closed toe shoe. I recommend Danskos, Clarks, Naturalizers, Crocs and Aerosols. You may have to try several in order to find the right pair for you.

Thank you and I hope to see you in the air soon!

Safe Travels...